ROOTS RUN DEEP
Africa to the Americas

Photographs copyright © 2020 Willard G. Taylor
Aphorisms and Text copyright © 2020 Albert G. Mosley

All rights reserved.

No part of this publication may be reproduced, stored in a retrieval system, or transmitted in any form or by any means, electronic, mechanical, photocopying, recording, scanning, or otherwise except as permitted by Section 107 or 108 of the 1976 United States Copyright Act, without the prior expressed written permission of the authors.
Request for the authors permission visit: www.rootsrundeep-thebook.com

BOOK DESIGN and LAYOUT: Willard G. Taylor

LIBRARY OF CONGRESS CATALOGING-IN-PUBLICATION DATA
Library of Congress Control Number: 2020909998

ISBN: 978-0-578-70225-4

First Printing, 2021

Published by:
YourWorld Consultant Group, Inc.

Printed in the United States of America
Signature Book Printing, www.sbpbooks.com

ROOTS RUN DEEP
Africa to the Americas

Willard G. Taylor Photographer

Albert G. Mosley Introduction and Aphorisms

CONTENTS

Roots Run Deep

9

Introduction

11

Aphorisms & Photographs

14

Acknowledgements

297

Authors

299

ROOTS RUN DEEP

In the course of my travels throughout the African world, many stories were voiced regarding the virtues of the Baobab Tree. Once, while traveling across the savannah lands of West Africa, I remember asking, "how can a tree survive out here?" I was told, "that is a Baobab Tree, their roots run deep and can extend for many kilometers from it's trunk. It can live for hundreds of years. The Baobab Tree is known as the Tree of Life. This tree serves many purposes. Its roots absorb and stores water during the rainy season and produce a nutritiously rich fruit during the dry season. This tree provides water, food and shelter for people and animals alike."

The African Diaspora, like the Baobab Tree, has roots that run deep and have extended for many miles across continents. The essence of our collective humanity has traveled along the paths of those roots and infused every element in defining who we are as a people.

Willard G. Taylor

INTRODUCTION

In another world and time
our thoughts bent within
the surface of our skins
until they broke the surface
with angry cries
and woeful grins
Born angry and lost
and cast upon a sky so bleak
told to carry on in spite
of the threats and entreaties
to retreat
We lifted our heads
and gave to all our energy
to move
the surface of our body
to move
the earth that covers God
within the hills and valleys
and rivers and creeks
and hearts of men

The primary insight of this work is in the continuity that exists between indigenous Africans and people of African descent in the Americas, and modes of expression. The photographs merge the people by shifting from Africa to the Americas and back, and as a people they become indistinguishable. In a similar manner, the aphorisms and photographs merge and hopefully, illustrate an important aspect of art forms in general, namely, that the significance of a situation is determined by the way in which it is presented and interpreted.

Traditional forms of community interactions are ever present in African culture; yet, such ties have been all but forgotten in much of the modern world. This is especially true of folk-art forms. Unlike in the modern world, where there is always a clear distinction between audience and performer, in traditional African life no such clear-cut distinction was possible. For enjoyment and enlightenment, one did not go to watch others perform. Rather, performers took turns performing amongst themselves, regardless of skill-level. A full appreciation of the impact of Africa on the evolution of western civilization awaits a clearer understanding of the role of the artist in articulating individual expression within the community.

Culture shapes and molds our feelings into patterns we spontaneously use to express ourselves. Using the movements, gestures, and sounds developed by our communities, we articulate our personal feelings and........in no place in the world are human expressions more vividly-articulated than in Africa. This photography is a testimony to the sensitivity of its people, despite differences of countries and continents.

When it is necessary to see a situation from a certain point-of-view, the appropriate proverb, or "saying," has traditionally served to make the point. Proverbs and aphorisms articulate perspectives on situations that are intended to affect how we feel and are disposed to act toward such situations in general. While present in every culture, they seem to play a very special role in African life. Spontaneously produced during the course of conversations, they define a tendency that is not to be ignored. For not only art, but science and morality as well, rest on the root ability of human beings to see things from different points of view. Illustrating this is certainly an enterprise where two heads are better than one.

Hopefully, the images we present will aid in dispelling the myth that people of African descent in the Americas have lost all connection with their African cultural roots. Our work is dedicated to the indispensably practical utility of verbal and visual perspectives on the human condition.

Albert G. Mosley

Musicians
    Create Rhythms
       Which Shape
          The Bodies
          of Dancers
       As Again
The Created
    Becomes
       The Creator

Cape Verde

USA

Brazil

Cuba

Cuba

Nigeria / USA

Cuba

Senegal

USA

Senegal

Cuba

Kenya

Cuba

Dominican Republic | Haiti

Cuba

Cuba

USA

Cuba

Cuba

USA

Brazil

Cuba

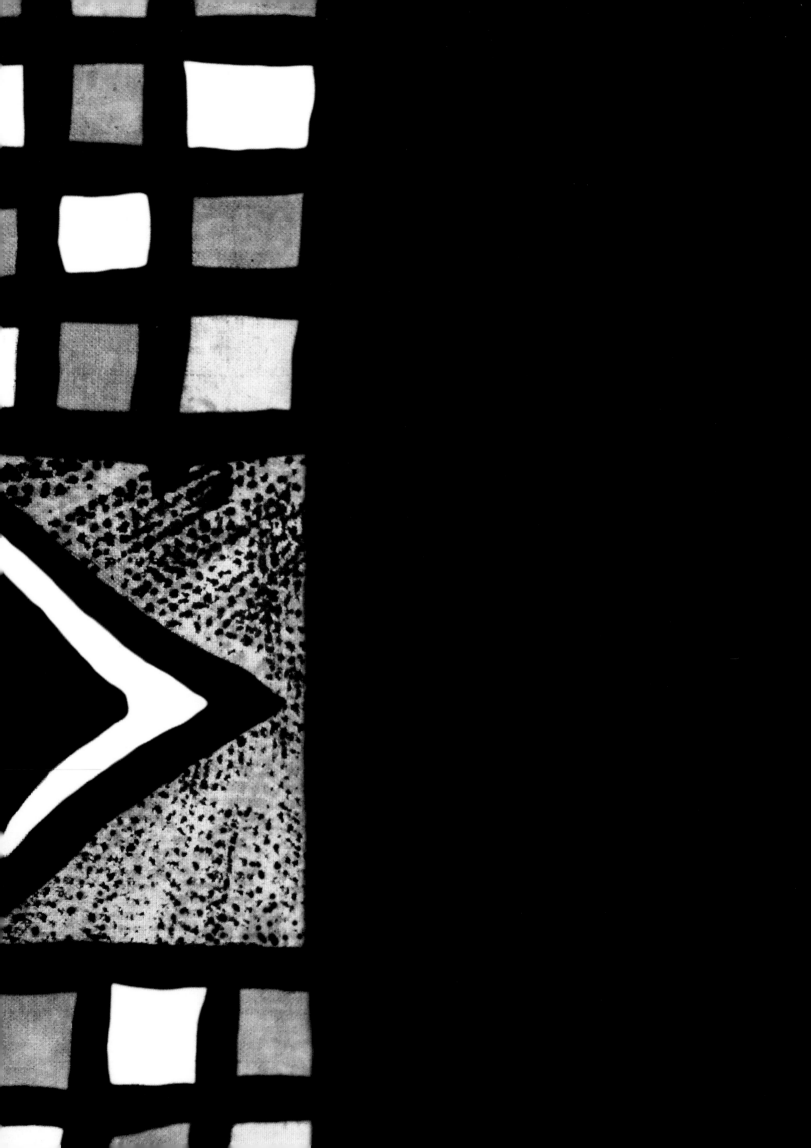

A Philosopher
Teaches Others
To Teach Themselves

Cyril Lionel Robert "C.L.R." James

Trinidad and Tobago

Cyril Lionel Robert "C.L.R." James

Trinidad and Tobago

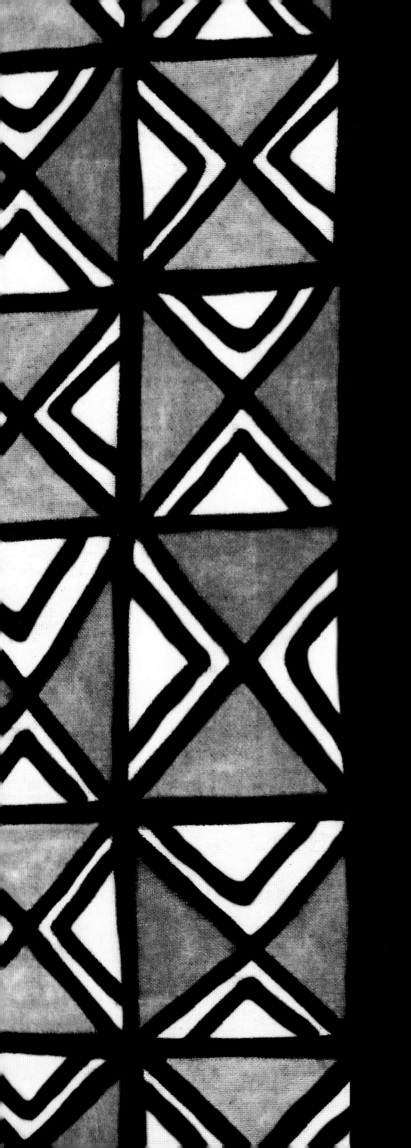

Children enjoy life
because they do not
worry about the consequences
of their actions

Brazil

USA

Brazil

USA

Cuba

USA

Dominican Republic

Kenya

USA

Senegal

Truth expressed
in a manner
inaccessible to
ordinary people
Is
Water presented
to a thirsty man
as vapor
in the air

Riley "B.B." King

USA

Allan "Mutabaruka" Hope

Jamaica

**Neguinho do Samba
(Antonio Luis Alves de Souza)**

Brazil

Banda Didá

Brazil

Phase II Pan Groove — Trinidad and Tobago

El Conga Guayabito — Cuba

Ray Charles Robinson

USA

Milton Nascimento

Brazil

Gilberto Gil Moreira

Brazil

Robert "Bobby Blue" Bland

USA

Orestes Macias

Cuba

Henry "Taj Majhal" Fredericks

USA

"Little"Esther Phillips

John Lee Hooker

USA

To Care
is
to share
your
world with
another

USA

Many make themselves
slaves
to a
method or creed
Thinking in this way
to make
Fate
their slave

Jamaica

The nature
 of a diamond
is not changed
 because a beautiful
woman
 comes to love it

Senegal

Truth
    Like herbal medicines
    Like the scapel of Surgeons
Can Injure or Heal

Ghana

You may have the answer
without recognizing that
it is your solution

Brazil

He to whom the
　　　Multitudes
are
　　　Indebted
will be boosted
　　　to
　　Immortality

Thurgood Marshall

USA

South Africa

Desmond Mpilo Tutu

Maura de Caldas

Colombia

James E. Cheek & Julius K. Nyerere

USA / Tanzania

Abdou Diouf

Senegal

Jesse L. Jackson, Sr.

USA

Shirley Chisholm

USA

Maria Olívia Santana

Brazil

Benjamin E. Mays

USA

Abdias do Nascimento

Sílvio Humberto dos Passos Cunha

Maria Raymunda Araújo

Brazil

Angela Yvonne Davis
USA

Makota Valdina Pinto
Brazil

Marta Cordiés Jackson
Cuba

Stevie Wonder – (Stevland H. Morris)

USA

Mãe Hilda Jitolu – (Hilda Dias dos Santos)
Brazil

Audley "Queen Mother" Moore
USA

Raiford C. "Ossie" Davis
USA

Mãe Stella de Oxóssi
(Maria Stella de Azevedo Santos)

Brazil

Jeremiah A. Wright, Jr.

USA

A child
becomes fully
an Adult

Only if

The child
has been fully
a Child

Ghana

Ghana

Ghana

Ghana

To move
one must learn
to alternate
between one's
different aspects

James Van Der Zee

USA

Ignorance
     is someone
not knowing
     what others
do know

USA

Colombia

Brazil

Cuba

Dominican Republic

Jamaica

USA

Brazil

Cuba

Success takes
    Root
in soil enriched
    by yesterdays Failures

USA

A moment is
    Pregnant
with unborn hours
    A day
with the labors
    of years

Ghana

Senegal

USA

Kenya

If the horse
      you are given
is too wild
      for you to tame
If the gold placed in
      your hands
is too heavy
      for you to carry
If the house
      for you to live in
is too large
      for you to fill
      you need help
you need help
      you need help

Senegal

The Will that
Shapes
    devices its
        own Methods

Cuba

Not everyone would do something
The way you would do it
Not everyone could do something
The way you could do it
Not everyone should do something
The way you should do it

Democratic Republic of the Congo

Do not confuse
what is right
with
who is right

Brazil

The test of life
is the ability to
Create

Babatunde Olatunji

Nigeria

Maxwell "Max" Roach

USA

Miles Dewey Davis III

John L. "Jackie" McLean

USA

Hermeto Pascoal

Brazil

**Hugh Ramapolo Masekela
& Mtutuzel Dudu Pukwana**

South Africa

Arthur "Art" Blakey

USA

Joseph "Joe" Kennedy Jr.

John Birks "Dizzy" Gillespie

Lee Morgan

William "Count" Basie

USA

Nina Simone - (Eunice Waymon)

Denise "Dee Dee" Bridgewater

The World Saxophone Quartet - David Murray, Julius Hemphill, Oliver Lake, and Hamiet Bluiett

USA

Randy Weston & (father) Frank Weston

USA

Walter "Sonny" Rollins
USA

Betty Carter
(Lillie Mae Jones)
USA

Hayes Burnett

USA

Wynton Marsalis

USA

Julio Valdés Fuentes

Cuba

Joatan Nascimento

Brazil

Abdullah "Dollar Brand" Ibrahim

South Africa

Sun Ra - (Herman Poole Blount)

Dexter Gordon

Charles "Charlie" Mingus Jr.

USA

Julius Arthur Hemphill
USA

Rahssan Roland Kirk
USA

Lester Bowie — USA

Carlos do Nascimento — Angola

Mother earth
    remains with and
sustains her children
    while God the father
rules from afar

Benin

Kenya

Cuba

Senegal

Ghana

One must be as
           Humble
As one is
           Powerful
If one is to use
           Strength
           Wisely

Muhammad Ali

USA

Muhammad Ali

USA

Widsom is
         knowledge gained
            through the pleasures and pains
of Human Existence

USA

Cape Verde

Ghana

Jamaica

Haiti

Trinidad and Tobago

Brazil

USA

Cuba

Ghana

Cuba

USA / Cuba

Kenya

USA

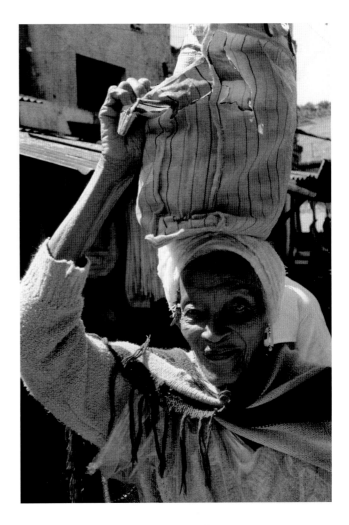

Brazil

Senegal

Thank God
my heart does not stop
simply when I think
for it to

What if
like my arm
it stopped when I told it to?

Thank God
my heart does not stop
simply when I think
to see what it
would do

USA

Brazil

Kenya   Haiti

Jamaica

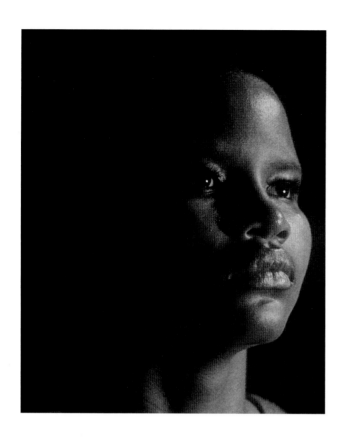

USA

You can touch
neither your Heart
nor the Sun
yet Both are
the Foundations
of Life

Cuba

You never know . . .
    You've waited too long . . .
        Un-
            till
                it's
                    too
                        late.
                            . .
                              . . .
                              . . .

USA

Patience
is the Key
to many Treasures

Cuba

A Pledge
   to make life
Better
   for another
Is not
   Fulfilled
In a day

Cuba

USA

So long as your aim is to help
You need not fear your own motivations

Cuba

Once you have
    knowledge
        you are
Held Responsible
    for using
it Wisely

Gwendolyn E. Brooks

USA

Tomás F. Robaina

Cuba

Kimbwandende Kia Bunseki Fu-Kiau

Democratic Republic of the Congo

Goli Guerreiro

Brazil

Mohamed Sesay

Sierra Leone

Gisela A. Covarrubias
Cuba

José Carlos Limeira
Brazil

Amiri Baraka
USA

James A. "Jimmy" Baldwin

USA

Raúl Ruiz Miyares

Cuba

Margaret A. Walker

USA

Radamés Giró

Cuba

Yosef A. A. Ben-Jochannan

USA

Like Strength
Wisdom
Can Only Be
Developed
Slowly

Cuba

Senegal

Brazil

Dominican Republic

USA

Brazil

Cuba

Colombia

Brazil

USA

Colombia

Cuba

Brazil

Dominican Republic

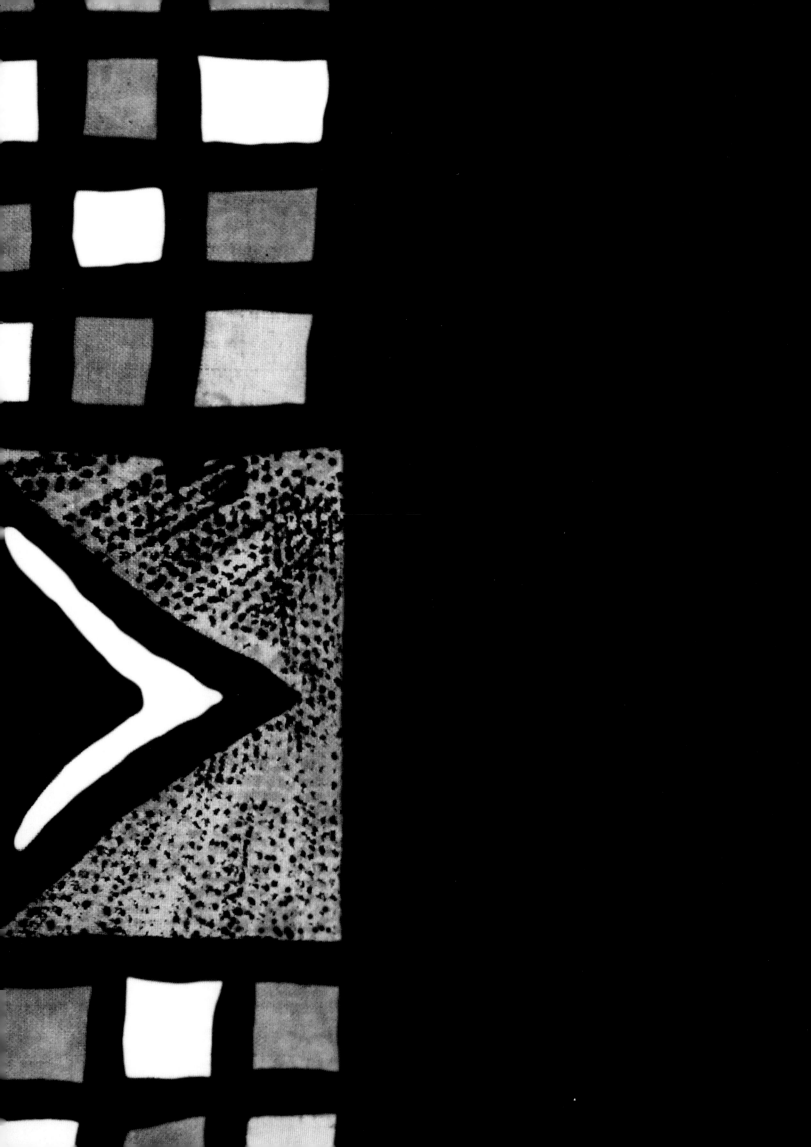

We give
    to the child
that we may
    receive from the adult

USA

Brazil

Brazil

Cuba

USA

Ghana

USA

Kenya

He who teaches by engaging in Slient Action
    Can hear while Speaking
    Can teach while Learning
    Can stalk while Standing
    Submit while Commanding

**Irmandade da Nossa Senhora da Boa Morte
(Sisterhood of Our Lady of the Good Death)**

Brazil

**Irmandade da Nossa Senhora da Boa Morte
(Sisterhood of Our Lady of the Good Death)**

Brazil

**Irmandade da Nossa Senhora da Boa Morte
(Sisterhood of Our Lady of the Good Death)**

Brazil

**Irmandade da Nossa Senhora da Boa Morte
(Sisterhood of Our Lady of the Good Death)**

Brazil

The Instinct
Without
The Act:
   Love unfilled
   Anger unpursed
   Joy without Laughter
   Sorrow without Tears

Cuba

To explore the Unkown
 at the risk of injury
  is the childlike nature
   of man

Dominican Republic

Democratic Republic of the Congo

Senegal

Do all
    that you are
capable of doing
    and You will know
how to motivate others

Kenya

When you do not know
      what the problem is
Its easy to believe
      there is no problem
When you do not know
      what the solution is
Its easy to believe
      there is no solution

USA

Changes will continue
    as long as there are people
    determined to conquer the
fear of having to change

Brazil

Kenya

Cuba

Through experience
we grow
To bear the
fruit of wisdom
At Maturity

USA Brazil

Ghana Cuba

On reflection
The most trival
And commomplace
Episodes
Of life
Furnish the most
Significant
of Truths

Elizabeth Catlett

USA

Januwa Moja Nelson
USA

Juan A. Picasso Cordero
Cuba

Domingos "Terciliano Jr." Alves Filho
Brazil

Louis Vergniaud Pierre-Noel & Lois Mailou Jones Pierre-Noel

Haiti / USA

Prentice Herman "P.H." Polk

James L. Wells, Sr.

Selma H. Burke

USA

Nike Okundaiye

Nigeria

William E. Carter

USA

Benny Andrews

Ernest Crichlow

Richard A. Long & David C. Driskell

USA

Norman W. Lewis

USA

Jacob Lawrence

USA

Salvador Gonzáles Escalona

Gloria Rolando Casamayor

Eduardo "Choco" Roca

Cuba

Alberto Lescay Merencio

Cuba

Margaret Taylor-Burroughs

USA

Romare Bearden

USA

Love
is
the Mother
of
Children

The milk
from which
our
Bones
are formed

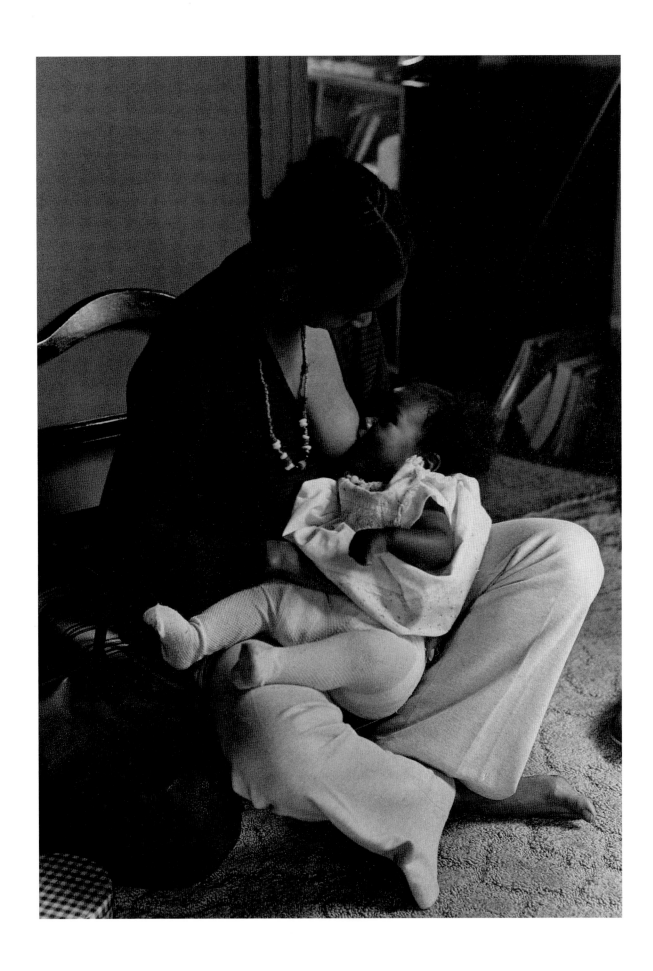

USA

Ghana

Kenya

Ghana

Cuba

Kenya

Cuba

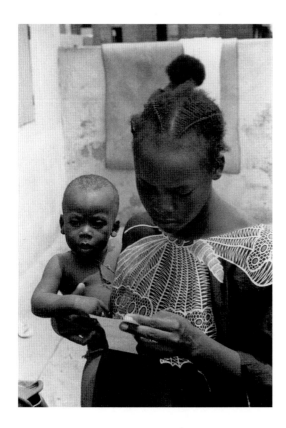

Senegal

Ghana

The same thing
　　can be expressed
In as Many Different Ways
　as there are Things
　Capable of expressing
　　themselves

Cuba

Brazil

Cuba

USA

Haiti

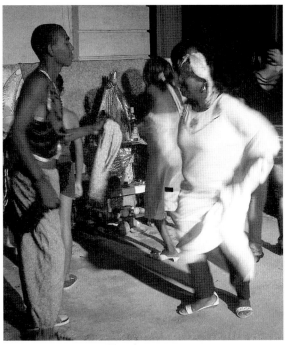

Cuba

USA

USA

Brazil

Jamaica

USA

USA

To prepare
for the future
            Live
the present
to the
Fullest

Brazil

USA

Brazil

U.S. Virgin Islands

Cuba

Brazil

Dominican Republic   U.S. Virgin Islands

Brazil

We Live
         through the Sacrificies
that Others
         have made

Senegal

It is not always best
	to get more
merely
	because
there is more to get

Trinidad and Tobago

Brazil

Without
  Inspiration
The least
  Obstacle
    Is
  Insurmountable

Cuba

Not to know is
not the same
as being incapable
of knowing

Kenya

The greater the number
    who share in my Cake
    the less there is
    for each
The greater the number
    who share in my Love
    the more there is
    for each

Senegal / USA

To Teach
    one must be constantly
        Learning
To Lead
    one must be carefully
        Following

Cuba

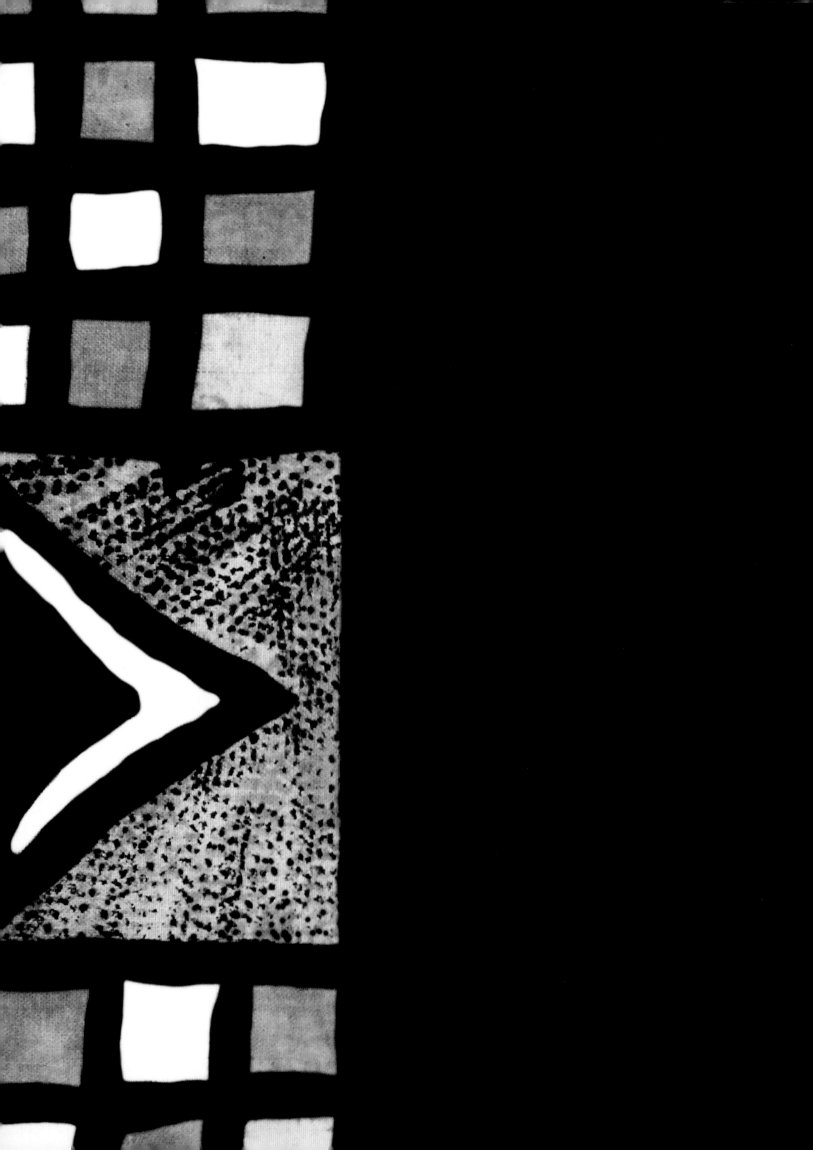

Will and determination
 makes thoughts into words
 and words into deeds

Kenneth D. B. Kaunda arrives at Whitehouse

Zambia / USA

Kenneth D.B. Kaunda departs the Oval Office

Zambia / USA

Kenneth D. B. Kaunda at Whitehouse State Dinner

Zambia / USA

Kenneth D. B. Kaunda meets with the Congressional Black Caucus

Zambia USA

Kenneth D. B. Kaunda addresses Luncheon at Department of State

Zambia / USA

A tree bears
   the hardships of
winter, storms, and abuse
   still to blossom
with flowers in spring
and fruit in the fall

Callejón de Hamel

Cuba

Callejón de Hamel

Cuba

Callejón de Hamel

Cuba

Callejón de Hamel

Cuba

Children
are
the products
of
Joy
where we
share
ourselves
with others

Jamaica

USA

If you have nothing
    except what you win
in the contests you enter
    the games you play
    then you have everything
    to lose
    and nothing to gain

Brazil

USA / Brazil

USA

USA / Brazil

We teach
 the dead
and the living
 through our actions
and decisions

Nigeria / USA

If you must
prepare
when the time
comes
the time will be
past

Ghana

Fear and Terror
> are Mother and Son
They mate
> to Agitate
> the World

Kenya

Work
When work is required
Fight
When fighting is necessary
Relax
When relaxation is possible

Senegal

By being tolerated
    We learn
To tolerate others
    By practing
Kindness
    We teach others
To be Kind

Cuba

The Goal
 I fall short of
  Will be reached
   By others
    Through my
     Efforts

Chuba Okadigbo

Nigeria

Maulana N. "Ron" Karenga

USA

Charlene M. Claye

USA

Juan Carlos Vaillant

Cuba

João P. "João Pequeno" dos Santos & João O. "João Grande" dos Santos

Brazil

Clarindo de Silva
Brazil

Zoe Creme Ramos
Cuba

John Asamoah
Ghana

Rigoberto Lopez

Cuba

Gilberto R. N. Leal

Brazil

Kwame Ture - (Stokely S.C. Carmichael) USA

Antônio C. "Vovô" dos Santos Brazil

Without Action
    A Blueprint of the
Future
Provides only ideas
    to Analyze

African Liberation Day

USA

African Liberation Day

USA

Human Rights

Jamaica

Marcha das Mulheres Negras contra o Racismo e a Violência

The Black Womens March against Racism and Violence

Marcha das Mulheres Negras contra o Racismo e a Violência

Brazil

**Marcha das Mulheres Negras
contra o Racismo e a Violência**

**Marcha das Mulheres Negras
contra o Racismo e a Violência**

Brazil

Million Man March

USA

Million Man March

USA

Million Man March

USA

Million Man March

USA

Every experience
has a thousand faces -
Where one encounters
the grotesque
another discovers
Beauty

Cuba

USA

Democratic Republic of the Congo

Brazil

Cuba

Ghana

USA

Colombia

Dominican Republic

Cuba

Nicaragua

Brazil

Ghana

Colombia

Brazil

Dominican Republic

Trinidad and Tobago

Cuba

293

All peoples of African descent, whether they live in North or South America, the Caribbean, or any other part of the world are Africans and belong to the African nation.
KWAME NKRUMAH

ACKNOWLEDGEMENTS

Our sincere gratitude to the individuals, organizations, and institutions who have supported us through the years that have made this book possible.

A special thanks to photographers Dexter Oliver and Joseph "Tex" Gathings who were my early mentors and instilled a solid foundation that served me throughout my photographic career.

We express our sincere gratitude to C. Daniel Dawson for his beautiful essay and the ongoing support and encouragement he provided throughout this journey.

Our deepest appreciation to Charlene Claye for her friendship, inspiration and wisdom during the preparation of this book.

AUTHORS

Albert G. Mosely is a Professor of Philosophy at Smith College in Northampton, Massachusetts. He has authored and co-authored two books: *African Philosophy and Affirmative Action: Social Justice or Unfair Preference?* His article, "Autobiographical Musings on Race, Caste, and Violence appeared in *Radical Philosophy Review*, a peer-reviewed forum for activist scholars, community activists, and artists. His most recently published philosophical essays are: "Music, Modernity, and Pragmatism"; "Racial Differences in Sports: What's Ethics Got to do With It?"; "African Philosophy at the Turn of the Century"; "Expanding the Moral Circle"; "From Racism to Speciesism"; "Should the Racial Contract Replace the Social Contract?"; and, "Science and Technology in Contemporary African Philosophy." He has also constructed reviews on books such as "Wonders of the African World" by Henry Louis Gates, Jr., and "An Introduction to African Philosophy" by Samuel Oluoch Imbo. Dr. Mosley was born in Dyersburg, Tennessee, received a BS in mathematics and a PhD in philosophy from The University of Wisconsin-Madison, and studied philosophy of science at Oxford University.

Willard G. Taylor is a professional photographer who practices in the areas of commercial and fine art photography. His work is displayed in a plethora of formats: CD, video, magazine covers, and album jackets, which span the United States, the Caribbean, Europe, Africa and South America. His fine art prints have been exhibited at national and international galleries in the U.S., Senegal and Brazil.

Taylor is currently the President and Founder of YourWorld Consultant Group, Inc., a special interest market research and development consultant company dedicated to serving groups and organizations interested in African Diaspora international educational programs, its culture and events. He served on several boards of directors including the Olatunji Center of African Culture, the Duke Ellington High School for the Arts in Washington, D.C. and the International Capoeira Angola Foundation. He has received numerous distinguished awards in the field of photography, including Time-Life Books - New Discovery (1977) and McMillian Publishers - The Complete Book of Photographers (1981). He has a Bachelor of Arts in Philosophy and Master of Science in Media Technology.